Leadership Life-style

A Staff Management Handbook

Leadership Life-style

A Staff Management Handbook

by
Denny Williams, D.B.A.

Beacon Hill Press of Kansas City
Kansas City, Missouri

Copyright 1983
by Denny Williams, D.B.A.

Printed in the United States of America

ISBN: 0-8341-0810-0

Cover Art: Royce Ratcliff

10 9 8 7 6 5 4 3 2 1

Preface 7

Acknowledgments 9

Introduction 10

1. Priority Approach
 Management 13
 Planning 15
 Organizing 17
 Staffing 19
 Directing 21
 Controlling 23
 The Bible and Management 25
 Time Management 27
 Committees 31
 Budgeting 33
 Goals 35
 Communication 37
 Leadership 39

2. Personal Style
 Assertiveness 43
 Delegating 45
 Human Relations 47
 Priorities 49
 Motivation 51
 Empathy 53
 Written Communication 56
 Executive Skills 58
 The Ultimate Example 60
 Success (Achievement) 62

Contents

Contents

3. Potential Problems
Stress 67
Inactive Members 69
Complainers 71
Procrastination 73
Conflict 76
Solutions 78

4. Promotional Strategy
Advertising 83
Ad Ideas 86
Newsletters 89
Helpful Hints 93
Plan Sheet 95

5. Personnel Structure
Hiring 99
Job Description 102
Staff Productivity 103
Secretaries 105
Personnel Handbook 108

6. Preventative Action
Creative Change 113
Policies 116
Growth 117
Development 119

Preface

Within the magnitude and scope of "management" lies the reality that God's method is men! It always has been and always will be. God simply takes you as a Christian leader, pastor, or worker, and ministers through your life to accomplish His purpose. Oftentimes, however, our great, mighty, all-knowing, all-powerful, unchanging, eternal, perfect, and personal God—has His hands tied! Frequently, He is limited by people! Not so sure? Notice, if you will, Ps. 78:41 where we read: "Yea, they [the children of Israel] turned back and tempted God, and *limited the Holy One of Israel*" (italics mine).

What a lesson for us today! To think that many Christian leaders are keeping God from blessing—actually hindering effective administration within their organizations! Are you blocking His perfect plan? You see, God has established order, direction, and conditions that must be met if you are to experience success in your ministry. Thus, when you neglect the *basic functions of management,* you are in effect tying God's hands.

Blockades to effective administration are countless, but the very basic ones can be summed up as:
1. **Presumption**—God is limited by pet phrases, empty definitions, canned methods, and unfounded expectations.
2. **Pride**—God resists the proud. Too many are self-made, self-centered, self-sufficient Christian leaders.

3. **Prejudice**—God is sometimes bound by traditions, methods, ideas, and personal prejudices which seem more important than biblical principles and management concepts.
4. **Personal Aspirations**—God is not impressed by the desire to enhance your reputation, increase your scope of ministry, or gain personal recognition for you from others in the field.
5. **Pretense**—God gets tired of professional phoniness which leaves a negative impression on others and reflects a poor image of Christ.

Because the children of Israel turned back, tempted God, and limited Him, God did not bless them. But the conclusion is what gives us cause for great rejoicing as Christian leaders. God "chose David also his servant . . . to feed Jacob his people, and Israel his inheritance. So he fed them according to the integrity of his heart; and guided them by the skilfulness of his hands" (Ps. 78:70-72).

God has given us the building blocks for successful administration and leadership life-style in His Word. You can build a strong leadership style by implementing the Bible along with the creative tools contained in this practical guide.

Acknowledgments

Unfortunately, most people who read and utilize the principles of *Leadership Life-style* will never have the opportunity to know the individuals who have contributed personally to the creation of this book. These are significant and special people to me:

Wayne and Bea Williams, my parents, who supported my educational aspirations

Sheila Goldsmith, my secretary, who typed the original manuscripts

Dr. F. R. "Dick" Cole, my pastor, who served as my professional advisor

Ron Burtraw, my professor, who recognized a unique concept and encouraged me

Gayle Hilligoss, my friend, who critiqued and typed the final manuscript

Dr. Casto Ball, my associate, who continually inspired my work through his life and example

Judy Williams, my wife, with whom I have had the joy of living out the principles of *Leadership Life-style*.

Introduction

Richard Innes once made the statement: "You only really believe that which motivates you." How true you will find this to be in society as you simply observe the people around you. From the extreme dedication of the Jehovah's Witness—to the commitment of the Communist—to the average American playboy, you can see that people are motivated by the standards and values of the heart.

Leaders persuade people! As a Christian leader, you are a vital part of the management process within the framework of the local church/organization. Your objective is to bring about a change in the values and concepts of others within your realm of responsibility. Many times the task of "persuasion" is a disappointing disaster.

Persuasion takes on many forms, with your attitudes changing as you are challenged. New attitudes are created or reinforced, while others neutralize. Sometimes there is no visible alteration or only a slight one, but given time and loving care, conversion takes place.

It's within this context that I have chosen to write *Leadership Life-style,* to share with you management principles for a more effective ministry. As you and I incorporate the powerful principles stated herein, along with the help of the Holy Spirit, our ministry will be even more successful (1 Cor. 14:40).

The future of any church/organization and its outreach depends largely upon management skills in relationship to *plans, programs,* and *people.* The essence of this nonexhaustive book is what God expects you to be—the very best!

1

PRIORITY APPROACH

MANAGEMENT

Management is a process! Whether you are a pastor, organizational leader, or committee chairman who desires greater results in your administration, you must first understand that you are a manager: that is, a supervisor, with a genuine focus on people.

According to one of my former associates, a good manager gets things done through and with people, motivating and guiding their efforts to accomplish stated objectives. It is imperative to have a plan of action for every area within the framework of your organization. Without such plans, you will not be as effective as God would have you be.

Management has five basic functions. Although sometimes given other titles, these functions remain basically the same. They are:

1. **Planning**—determining ways and methods in which a particular act, goal, or project can be executed, based on past and present data, plus financial resources.

2. **Organizing**—coordination of plans, programs, and people in a harmoniously united action—teamwork.

3. **Staffing**—maintaining the best-qualified people in leadership roles to help plan, administer, and execute operational plans and schedules.

4. **Directing**—the ability to superintend, govern, and manage people in carrying out plans and programs.

5. **Controlling**—the ability to check, regulate, exercise restraint, give direction, and oversee the entire system.

I think you will agree that a most important and least implemented function is oftentimes *planning*. Many simply fail to plan! Somehow you let people steal your time and/or allow them to impose outside time frames on you. For various reasons, you accomplish little, as "forest fire emergencies" consume any fragment of leftover available time.

Here is how you can plan effectively and get results:

1. **Write it down**—Make a list so you can visualize the entire situation. This list should become your own personal "To Do" list.
2. **Categorize**—Rearrange your list, placing the most important items first. It is too easy to spend time on less meaningful matters.
3. **Classify**—Determine what must be done! As you prioritize and sort, you will accomplish the most difficult tasks before you become mentally and physically drained by the end of the day.
4. **Delegate**—Learn to give up some tasks. Allow others to use *their abilities* and at the same time relieve yourself of a number of tasks you may be needlessly burdened with. Herein lies one of the greatest threats to good management, because so often we would rather *do it ourselves*.

The ultimate purpose of good and successful management is *to get results!* Within our complex society, you must learn to coordinate your resources and surround yourself with strong people. Jesus is our ultimate Example. He put managerial concepts into a daily life-style. With effort, and application of the above principles, you have the tools to become a more creative manager.

PLANNING

Planning is the primary management function. It is only through planning that you can prepare to act in an uncertain society with little spiritual commitment.

Within the process of planning we have what are known as the "five Ps": purpose, philosophy, premises, policies, and plans. Your governing board, pastor, executive director, or council members may engage in strategic planning, and are therefore primarily responsible for the first four. Thus, organization members are given a general idea of what they are supposed to be doing and how it is to be accomplished. Plans, on the other hand, translate the general information into specific objectives and modes of action. Plans zero in on the *how, what,* and *when!*

The most effective planning in any organization begins at the top and works its way down. At least three levels of management usually exist, with three types of planning. The upper level staff takes care of strategic planning, the middle level employee carries out the intermediate planning, and the lower level (usually volunteer) formulates specific operational plans. Each lower level of planning becomes more detailed and covers a shorter span of time.

Strategic planning is vital, but often abused. Basically it involves the identification of your opportunities and barriers, both now and future. It also includes the identification of your organization's strengths and weaknesses and the establishing of priorities. The final benefit of strategic planning should be a firm conviction that your organization is doing the right thing, at the right time, with the right people.

Following strategic planning is the formulation of a planning system, beginning with proper objectives. Overall objectives at each level of planning should specify *what* the intended outcome is, *when* it is to be achieved, and *how* it can be *measured*. Your planning process needs to be completed by writing "action statements" that spell out *how* each objective is to be reached.

A number of techniques have been developed to aid the Christian leader in the planning process. Of course, one can hardly implement a particular method to fit all needs. Analyze your organization, seek staff appraisals, listen to employees and volunteers, examine successful organizations like your own and seek the counsel of other professionals. As you begin to plan and project, God's Spirit will strengthen your sensitivity and help your organization develop the best approach.

ORGANIZING

"Getting your act together" is not always easy. Organizing is a process of forming interdependent coordinated parts into a whole, for harmonious and united action. Remember, your organization is a social unit that is deliberately constructed and reconstructed in order to achieve specific objectives for the mutual benefit of all. In fact, every organization, whatever its purpose or reason for being, is characterized by:
1. Coordination of effort
2. A common goal or purpose
3. A work force (volunteers)
4. Levels of authority

The primary purpose of an organization may be business, nonprofit service, mutual benefit, or public function. In some respects all organizations share the same interests, while on the other hand, the various aspects of organizing may present you with unique problems and challenges.

To better organize, you should keep in mind the ever present *group concept* found in organizational structure. A group is more than a collection of people. People must freely interact and share a common identity and purpose before they become a group. Once you establish a cohesiveness (a "we" feeling), you will enhance your ability to insure continued organizational success.

A further step in organizing more effectively is your understanding of *group dynamics,* which refers to the constant activity and change within groups. There are three basic dimensions of group dynamics:

1. Roles
2. Norms
3. Interaction

A *role* is a predetermined prescription for behavior in a specific position. *Norms* tell you about what is right or wrong about your general behavior. (Both roles and norms strongly influence behavior.) *Interaction* plays a key role in organizational formation and development, since those who come together to share common activities must interact.

Group dynamics relates to better organizing because it can either help or hinder your total organization. Cohesiveness has proven to be a "two-edged sword." When the members of your organization want to accomplish a major task, they (by faith) will prove to be successful as they pull together. On the other hand, nothing will be done when the cohesive members decide not to act.

Organizing, then, takes time and understanding. To be effective, as you formulate where you want to be, you must feel the heartbeat of your people. Any form of construction is nothing more than hard work. Organizing is no exception. As you set the right forms, pour the cement, lay the proper bricks, and build your organization, God will bless your efforts!

STAFFING

Staffing involves planning which allows you to obtain and properly train key people for specific positions within your organization. There is little chance your organization will accomplish its intended purpose without being staffed by appropriately talented and motivated individuals.

The first factor in staffing is to obtain an adequate selection of candidates qualified to fill your vacant position. Keep in mind that there is a close relationship between the size of your candidate file and the effectiveness of your selection.

Another factor to consider is the motivation of the candidate. Individuals join organizations for a wide variety of reasons including: security, support, and opportunity for growth. Once you discover the motivational drive of your prospective candidate and seek to satisfy his basic needs, you are likely to have an active, involved, and committed employee. Your purpose is to create a comprehensive exchange involving more than the trading of a salary for services rendered. Therefore, don't stifle your staff's natural gifts and future growth.

An additional consideration is "human resource planning." In this process, you should assess your present staffing needs, forecast future needs, and formulate a staffing strategy. Occasional evaluation is necessary to keep your strategy updated. The final result should be the right person in the right position at the right time.

As you work through the proper channels and/or a personnel committee, you will have to give consideration whether to hire someone from the outside or seek to promote from within. (Modification and alterations to your present positions might need to be made by promoting within.) When selecting candidates from the outside, your attention will focus on recruitment and screening. Recruitment is the process of *identifying* those who are available for the position; while screening *separates* the qualified candidates from unqualified through interviews, reference checks, and committee evaluation. Selection should be based on accurate facts about the candidate in retrospect of the position to be filled.

A final factor of staffing involves actual job performance (see section on staff productivity). In order to promote someone within, you must consider and evaluate the individual's performance, because it will help or hinder the future course of your organizational direction. Plainly stated, compensation is closely tied to performance levels and does have an adequate motivational impact. Eternal rewards may be the ultimate desire of many Christian employees, while food and clothing remain essential to their effectiveness. Your concern and influence could very well make the difference for both now and eternity.

DIRECTING

Directing involves influencing or inducing your employees to a behavioral style designed to produce the greatest results. By directing, you focus on the motivation of work and attempt to obtain maximal contribution to your organizational goals. Directing, then, is concerned with motivation that achieves the highest levels of performance possible.

A number of concepts and terms (with a variety of meanings) are used in management circles, but the word *influence* best describes the process of directing. Influence refers to any behavior on the part of one individual which alters the behavior, attitudes, and feelings of another. Thus, a major concern in your management style is the way you influence (direct) your people in light of what you want to accomplish.

Two aspects of *managerial behavior* that are most commonly related to your immediate responsibility of directing are: (1) consideration and (2) initiating. *Consideration* refers to aspects of your behavior which indicate friendship, mutual trust, respect, and interpersonal warmth between you and your employees. *Initiating* refers to aspects of your behavior which organize and define employee (volunteer) activities and relationships, establishing clear patterns of work flow, channels of communication, and ways of accomplishing work loads.

Your success is dependent upon your example. You must guide your people through the maze of everyday obstacles within the framework of your organization. With proper instruction and plenty of the right information, your influence will produce the desired results in others.

Ask God to strengthen your ability to direct as you point out the way!

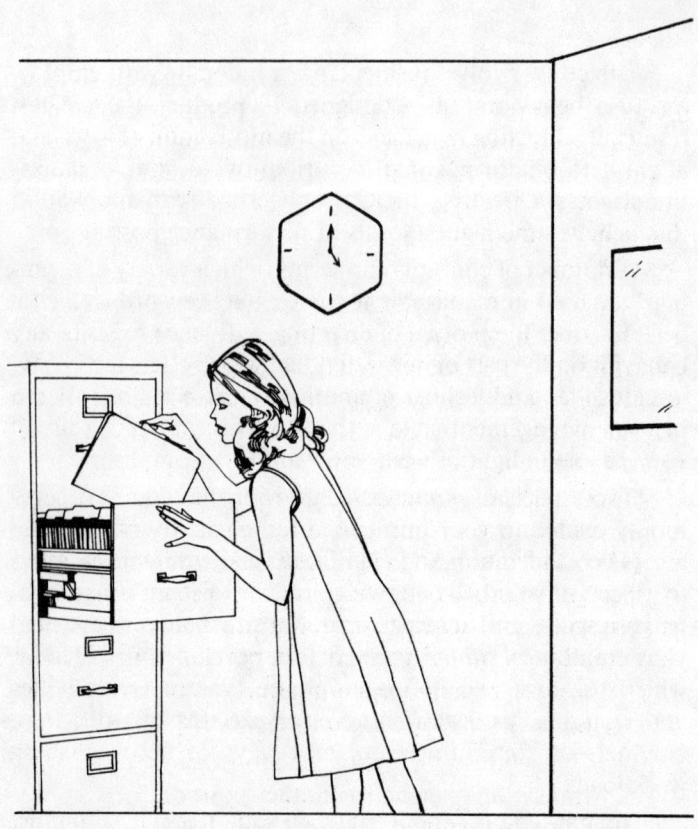

CONTROLLING

Managerial control is closely tied to planning. It enables you to be effective in both the near and distant future. Since plans sometimes fail, control is a vital complement to planning. As a creative manager, you exercise control by making adjustments to insure that your objectives are met as effectively and efficiently as possible. For most organizations the key areas of control are inventory, services, and financial stability.

One of the most widespread applications of control occurs in the area of individual performance. Your organization and staff have established certain acceptable levels which define effective performance. Below these levels the failures are considered extreme and indicate the type of action you should take to correct the situation.

Once you have established and identified the causes of poor performance by analysis, the next step in the control process is to determine which factors can and which cannot be changed. Also, a determination of whether a particular change will be sufficient to correct performance is essential. Thus, a strategy for corrective action develops.

A number of appropriate alternatives are available for you to use in the managerial control process:

1. Change the structure of the job.
2. Transfer the person to another position.
3. Properly train and develop the individual.
4. Make changes in supervision and compensation.
5. Modify personnel policies.

6. Counsel with the person about his/her performance.
7. Seek proper input and feedback.

Controlling your organization is vital to overall success. No one carries a greater responsibility to his staff associates, employees, and membership than you do. God has placed you in this key position to carry out His purpose—so take control and go for it.

THE BIBLE AND MANAGEMENT

The structure of management principles within the local church is based upon 1 Cor. 14:40 where the writer, Paul, exhorts: "Let all things be done decently and in order." (A good motto for any business!) In general, this concept is being carried out in the church, but often with little depth. Somehow, the leadership of your organization must seek to draw upon the resources already mentioned, begin to establish goals, and carry out the management process.

Here is a pattern for establishing the proper method of management for a church within the guidelines of the Bible:
1. God—Owner and Father
2. Minister/Ex. Director—Shepherd and Manager (Eph. 4:11)
3. Deacon/Board Member—Supervisor (1 Tim. 3:1-13)
4. Congregation—Employees and Ambassadors (2 Cor. 15:18-20)
5. Local Community
6. Four Corners of the Earth

It is within the area of "outlook" that many leaders stumble! Most simply fail to maintain the high standard expected or to fully grasp the concept for the method of management.

I'm not suggesting that you establish an autocratic leadership style or create a dictatorial empire. (There are too many skull busters out there now.) But I do advocate that God has placed ministers and leaders as shepherds who should manage their flocks with sensitivity and firmness. It is difficult to set up the structure that the illustration suggests, but not impossible. With a genuine love for all subordinates, a well-balanced atmosphere of control will blossom to the glory of God.

Management is a process! Any process takes time. Getting things done through and with people demands a positive outlook on behalf of all leaders. Approaching any topic of management in this age of complexity and pressure is a challenge. To relate such to God's Word and His expectations is basically unpopular, but for those who have been called to carry out the work of the church, there is an inner strength that comes from the Spirit of God.

TIME MANAGEMENT

WHAT IS TIME? (24 hours or 1,440 minutes)

Time is the raw material out of which life is built.

Time is gain for personal growth or great loss.

Your personal success (or lack of it) is largely contingent upon the effective use of your time!

Time is a perishable resource and must be used as a daily ration.

WHAT IS MANAGEMENT?

Management is a process!

Management is the process of getting things done through and with people to accomplish stated objectives.

Management is planning, organizing, staffing, directing, and controlling.

The ultimate purpose of good management is to *get results!*

WHAT IS TIME MANAGEMENT?

Time management is the process of reaching stated objectives by effectively using the least amount of time.

The key to time management is self-discipline. Ultimately it is the person, not the process, that will determine success or failure in the use of time.

The management of time is a lifelong process. No other investment pays higher dividends.

Since there are never enough hours in the day for everything you need or want to do, it is essential that you manage your time as efficiently as possible. Here are two principles that will dramatically increase your usable time:

1. Concentrate on what's most important for you to do.
2. Delegate all other tasks to your staff and employees.

To determine what is most important, you must re-analyze your operational structure and overall goals. Christ is the pivotal point around whom your activities should revolve. Anything that does not contribute to attaining your ultimate goal is a potential *time waster.*

NAME			SAMPLE TIME LOG			DATE
TASKS:		MONDAY	TUESDAY	WEDNESDAY	THURSDAY	FRIDAY
1.	9:00					
2.	9:30					
3.	10:00					
4.	10:30					
5.	11:00					
6.	11:30					
7.	12:00					
8.	12:30					
LONG RANGE PROJECTS	1:00					
1.	1:30					
2.	2:00					
3.	2:30					
4.	3:00					
5.	3:30					
6.	4:00					
7.	4:30					
8.	5:00					

For several weeks, keep a daily time log of everything you do and the time involved. This will *help you identify* the following major time wasters:

1. Interruptions and who/what causes them
2. Time-consuming tasks which should be delegated to others
3. Unscheduled functions which should be consolidated into specific time periods

Many experts stress the importance of complete honesty and accuracy in keeping your time log. You'll be surprised when you see the amount of wasted time recorded for days which you thought were crammed full of productive activities. It is easy to waste a couple of hours a day engaging in unrelated conversations, reading irrelevant materials, and receiving unnecessary telephone calls.

To eliminate most time wasters, you must *become aware of them*. Phone calls can be screened, and you can cut short unnecessary calls. Ask your secretary to handle routine calls and take messages when you need to be uninterrupted.

Unexpected visitors can be handled in several ways. Simply explain that you are busy, but that you'll give them 10 minutes now or schedule a longer appointment at another time. Or, you can remain standing while these people are in your office. This indicates that you have another appointment or something more pressing to do. Others have found that a clock on their wall relates the importance of *your time* and its true value.

Save your paper work and phoning for specific periods set aside for these purposes. You will save time by completing this work at one sitting, while you eliminate the hassle of beginning something, only to be interrupted again.

If you are serious about keeping a time log, you will discover wasteful patterns in your behavior of which you are unaware. Take, for example, the amount of time spent on across-town trips. By consolidating them into one day, with three or four consecutive stops, you will save a great deal of time on the road.

Notice the times of day when you appear to slow down and when you have excess energy. If your energy level is highest in the morning, schedule your most important tasks during the early hours and your least important tasks during your low energy period. If you are a slow starter but a real powerhouse in the afternoon, schedule your day accordingly.

Assigning Priorities is imperative! Make sure you're devoting the bulk of your time to tasks which contribute the most to your major goals. Establish the habit of maintaining a daily list of priorities.

Identifying Priorities is essential! The priority status of any task is usually based on two factors: urgency and importance. Only when the urgency is important to your objectives should it become a top priority item for you. Make a list.

Ranking Priorities on a scale of 1 to 10 is vital! Those both urgent and important should be numbered as top items. Those important but not urgent should be numbered next in sequence until you reach your least important tasks. All other duties are *secondary* to those on your priority list.

A final way to better manage your time is to *get other people to do secondary tasks.* As you evaluate that time log, identify those tasks that could easily be delegated (see "Delegating"). As you share the load and manage that valuable time, you will excel as a leader in your ministry.

COMMITTEES

If you don't accept and utilize the committee process within your organization, you will not succeed!

Most organizations function with two types of committees: *standing* and *special.* Standing committees usually deal with the ongoing programs, while special committees act on short-range projects.

The success of any committee depends upon its leadership and the committee members as a whole. Whatever the process of selection, be sure they are chosen according to their qualifications. Here are some suggestions:

1. Seek those who are interested and excited about the work to be done.
2. Seek out the visionary individual.
3. Seek the harmonious person who works well with others.
4. Seek to appoint those who are already faithful in service and programs.
5. Seek out the individual who has the proper priorities and enough time to serve effectively.

The overall results of any committee depend upon the leader or the chairman. Your ideal is to obtain an individual who fits most, if not all, of the above qualifications, since no committee will ever be better than its chairman. Thus, you need to encourage the selection of a chairman who is a natural leader with motivational ability to get members actively involved. His personal interest and knowledge of the committee's purpose is also essential.

A second factor of success for any committee is the basic understanding of its function or purpose. Upon appointment, a committee should know what work needs to be performed, the limitations established, and when their duties will be finalized. Take the time to talk with the committee chairman and clearly outline what is expected, or confusion may eventually crumble weeks of dedicated work.

Another factor of committe success is the continual flow of work which must be undertaken between regular meetings by designated members. An effective chairman will activate each person by making assignments and periodically checking the progress of each one.

A final success factor for a committee is the actual meeting. The date and time must be adequately communicated; the individual members should anticipate time for sharing; and the chairman needs to be well prepared with a printed agenda. The well-organized meeting will set the stage for greater accomplishment during the life of any committee.

Apply these principles and watch your committee results improve!

BUDGETING

Your budget is a financial plan!

Like a household budget, your organizational budget is a detailed plan of how funds will be spent, as well as how they will be obtained. Furthermore, your budget, when prepared properly, can be used to exercise control over various ministries. Thus, budgeting is a "tool" of management used for planning and control.

At the heart of the budgeting process is the basic concept of improving operations so you can accomplish your ministerial objectives in the most efficient way. Budgeting is not a device for limiting expenditures, but a tool which should give you the most productive and effective use of your organizational resources. A further asset of this tool is the realization that your budget is a valuable guide. A well-formulated budget will give your people a realistic understanding of the nature and purpose of your ministry. Plus, you will be effective and react quickly to developing events with a clear, concise budget.

Here are a few budgeting hazards to be aware of and to avoid:

1. Your programs may grow to such extremes that they become a burden. Overbudgeting is very dangerous.
2. Your staff may become pressurized and somewhat resentful, causing the defeat of your basic objectives.
3. Your people may sense greater demand on finances and thus lose sight of organizational goals.

4. Your inefficiencies may be hidden over a period of time, if you fail to evaluate.

A budget, then, will improve internal coordination as a planned allocation of your organizational resources, based on future predictions (forecasts). Forecasts are *necessary* in your ministry, so determine to analyze your financial system soon.

A key to success in your ministry is the proper use of management's tool—a budget.

		Page -3-
249	Adult Ministry - $2,150.00	$ 4,000.00
	The Senior Adult Ministry provides a way for the older adults of our church to have fellowship and activities that are meaningful and inspirational. The account includes ministry for the median adult years for department fellowships and outreach projects.	
250	SERVICE MINISTRIES - $58,594.00	49,466.00
251	Recreation - $2,770.00	2,000.00
	This item provides for equipment and fees related to athletic programs within the church.	
251A	Fellowship Committee - $500.00	500.00
	The Fellowship Committee provides receptions of various kinds for the church membership and plans the annual staff-deacon banquet each year.	
252	Media Center - $2,404.00	2,055.00
	The Media Center provides library services, tract distribution and audio-visual assistance to the church membership.	
253	Printing - $14,000.00	10,536.00
	Without the media of the printed page, a church would have a difficult task to communicate. This item includes all paper and printing supplies necessary to communicate the church's programs and ministries.	
254	Office and Organization Supplies - $4,800.00	3,000.00
	These supplies are required in the normal operation of the church office and related organizational supplies	
255	Public Relations - $3,200.00	2,900.00
	Advertising helps communicate the church's programs. Such items include newspaper, billboards, yellow pages and other media.	
256	Postage - $6,000.00	6,500.00
	This pays for office mailings, general organization stamps and provides funds for mailing the Advance and all bulk mailouts.	
257	Transportation - $4,000.00	3,000.00
	This provides for fuel, service and repairs for all church-owned vehicles.	
258	Word and Way - $800.00	650.00
	Word and Way is the official Missouri Baptist news magazine and is mailed to each family of our church who requests it.	
259	Food Service - 0	-0-
	The Wednesday Night Fellowship Service is the principal objective of this line item. Those who participate pay for the foodstuffs, thus -0- is budgeted. Related personnel expenses are cared for in the Salary Division of the budget.	
259A	Computer Services - $15,420.00	13,600.00
	Maintaining membership files for our 3500 members is a major responsibility. This account provides the resource to effectively and accurately keep up with the total membership plus sending envelopes and tabulating contribution	
		2,500.00
		825.00

GOALS

A goal is a future state of affairs that an organization or individual is trying to realize.

I believe it was Nichols Butler who in essence said that there are basically three kinds of people in the world: the many who simply don't know what is happening; those who only watch what is actually happening; and most vital, the few people who really *make things happen!* Jesus Christ is the example of a good manager, for He knew how to make things happen! He set His goals and sought to do the Father's will, changing the entire course of mankind.

GOALS HELP US MAKE THINGS HAPPEN!

Sit back and relax ... now close your eyes ... take a deep breath ... block out everything else in your mind ... and in one concise sentence, construct in a matter of minutes your ultimate goal in life.

It is sad to see in our society millions of people who are wandering around in the world without a goal or purpose in life. Millions do not know why they are here, what they are doing, or where they are going. They, like Moses and the children of Israel, are stumbling as if in the dark, without a future in sight, wandering aimlessly with little direction. You can be the "best" by setting goals within your organization and for yourself as well.

Your well-ordered life will require various levels of goals before a future state of affairs becomes a reality. Here are a few:

1. **Primary Goal**—your ultimate, overall purpose
2. **Real Goal**—what the majority of your resources are used for
3. **Stated Goal**—what you say your goal is, when in fact it might be something else in practice
4. **Short-term Goal**—when you make only one move at a time
5. **Long-term Goal**—the process of making many moves over a long period of time

Our churches are social units deliberately constructed and reconstructed to meet specific goals for the mutual benefit of all. A collective conscience is formed within the organization, a set of beliefs, sentiments, and values which is held in common by all members. If you fail to create a positive consciousness, it is doubtful you will be effective in reaching your goal.

Goals do at least four things:
1. Provide direction
2. Serve as motivators
3. Contribute to the overall management process
4. Act as the basis of philosophy

Without goals, the above are virtually absent from our daily administration, thus the failure of setting goals and accomplishing more rests entirely upon you. Blunt as it may sound, *the lack of goal setting is your fault!*

In summary, can we assume that the reason so many organizations fall short of their desired ministry is because they have failed to establish goals. As a leader, you can—you must—you *will* make things happen!

TO AIM AT **SOMETHING** AND MISS
IS BETTER THAN AIMING AT **NOTHING**
AND HITTING IT!!

COMMUNICATION

Communication is the imparting and interchange of thoughts, opinions, information, or instruction.

The process of communication is basically accepted within the framework of the following elements:

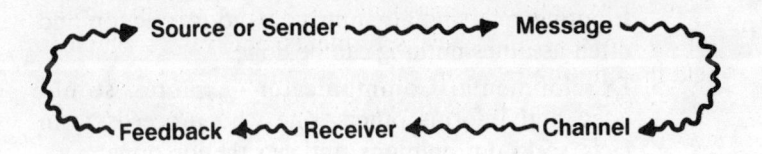

Source or Sender → Message → Channel → Receiver → Feedback →

Variations may occur, but usually these stages take place when you communicate, which means every element must be functioning properly to be effective. With proper implementation of the above, three changes take place in the areas of attitude, knowledge, and behavior.

At times you may encounter barriers in your communication. Usually, these barriers or breakdowns are caused by noise, status, ego, personal feelings, prejudices, and resistance to change. Many times the language used, physical conditions, or even your own experiences may be at fault. *Greater than any other barricade is the lack of shared meaning within the context of communication.* Sometimes we share different views and opinions with a stubborn attitude, failing to listen to what others are trying to say. There must be a sense of unity within your organization that is retained by good, positive, and open channels of communication.

In my past experience, I have seen the following styles of communication:

1. Controlling Communicator—uses persuasive force and pressure tactics; one who tells rather than sells.
2. Relinquishing Communicator—gives in to someone else and makes very few contributions; one who hates to exercise authority.
3. Accommodating Communicator—changes personal views to fit those of others; one who sets aside convictions and gives up all his power.
4. Withdrawing Communicator—simply stops contributing; one who attempts to avoid interaction and often assumes nothing can be done.
5. Developmental Communicator—explores, stimulates, and informs others; one who proceeds from facts, seeks out opinions, and gets the job done!

Now, need I say anything about these styles or which one you ought to be? Many leaders jump around in their style seeking different approaches, when in fact the only productive communicator is a developmental person.

A successful communicator anticipates feedback from others. Like a barometer, feedback indicates how effectively you have been communicating. Since approximately 85 percent of all communication is nonverbal, it should be no surprise that feedback is often nonverbal, as well as verbal: positive, negative, immediate, or delayed. With this in mind, let's learn to communicate with greater zeal, asking God to intercede for us. The point is to maximize your impact!

LEADERSHIP

Leadership is the ability to persuade others to seek defined objectives enthusiastically! A good leader will possess these distinct characteristics:
1. Swift and clear decision-making ability
2. Good listening ability
3. Motivational and directional skills
4. Basic knowledge of many different jobs
5. Ability to interact effectively with people
6. Skill in building teamwork and enthusiasm
7. **Vision** and ability to make things happen

The above qualities are basic for successful management, and it is essential to have a handle on each area to effectively persuade people.

Leaders play four basic roles. First of all, you are a builder of skills and developer of individual potential; secondly, you act as an advisor and director; the third role is that of appraiser and dispenser of justice; while your final role consists of being a spokesman and source of information.

It is within the framework of this fourth role that so many fail. Great tribulation creeps into any organization almost every time this area is overlooked. Get this down, for it is a concept that will completely change your ministry as a leader when applied in daily administration. Here it is: *Information Reduces Anxiety!* That's right! The more you keep your staff and people informed, the less anxiety you will encounter, and thus your effectiveness will increase.

Probably the most important aspect of being a successful leader is the ability to make swift and clear decisions. Strive for more *effective* thinking, rather than *perfect* thinking. And never underestimate the input and participation of others in the decision-making process.

Here are four personal factors of effective decision making:

1. Frame of reference (accumulated knowledge/experience)
2. Ability to process information and organize it
3. Personal value system and moral standards
4. Objectivity or degree to which you view yourself

Within the management structure (at least in educational circles) there is a widely accepted decision-making process known as the scientific method. Herein lies a secret to your future leadership success, as you learn to: (1) recognize and define the problem; (2) gather all the information; (3) form tentative conclusions; and (4) test those conclusions by gauging the results.

The Christian must be a dynamic leader in these last days of apostasy. With the aid of this practical guide, the Word of God, and the power of the Holy Spirit, you can become the administrator God wants you to be—beginning right now!

2

PERSONAL STYLE

ASSERTIVENESS

Assertiveness is "in" today! Behaviorists have discovered that assertiveness pays off in all areas of life. The Christian world is no exception.

To determine if you are assertive, you must be able to recognize two alternative kinds of behavior:

1. **Nonassertiveness**—is when you try to be overly nice, always wanting to be liked and shunning conflict. You're unable to say no without feeling guilty. In brief, this approach is emotionally dishonest because you deny your true feelings.
2. **Aggressiveness**—is when you pride yourself on being extremely tough. As an aggressive person, you try to dominate others, even if it means being hostile or insulting to them. You have little or no patience for their weaknesses, will rarely show concern for their feelings, and never admit to your own doubts or mistakes.

Assertiveness is the happy medium between the extremes of aggressiveness and nonassertiveness. It's based on respect for others' feelings and opinions, as well as your own. The assertive individual doesn't try to intimidate others. Neither does he subordinate his wishes to theirs or conceal his true feelings. On the contrary, he knows he has certain rights and he exercises them fairly.

If you are an assertive leader, you will:
1. Speak honestly and directly

2. Have strong ideas, yet listen to others
3. Have a good self-image (without perfection)
4. Not be afraid to admit mistakes
5. Not be afraid to change your mind
6. Know when to take a stand and when to compromise
7. Consider consequences without being paralyzed by fear
8. Not take criticism personally

Even with an assertive approach, you won't always be able to do what you want. Nobody can. But you will be able to build an honest, open relationship with your staff and co-laborers. Plus, you will achieve enough of what you are after to know you are in control and to feel good about yourself.

Tips for greater assertiveness:

1. Choose the right time and place to discuss a major issue.
2. Get your listener's attention by speaking positively.
3. State what you want clearly and directly without fear.
4. Take personal responsibility for your message.
5. Speak specifically. Don't assume others know what you mean.
6. Repeat your request by slightly rephrasing your point.
7. Ask questions to clarify how well you are understood.
8. Allow your manner, speech, and gestures to back up your words.

The above steps should help reduce communication gaps and increase response to your requests. Their effectiveness depends on your applying them.

DELEGATING

Delegation is a process used in distributing work to your staff and organizational members. The ability to skillfully delegate tasks is a key to success in a leadership life-style. Delegating involves these three steps:
1. The assignment of the task to a staff member
2. The relinquishing of authority to carry out the task
3. The involvement of that individual who assumes responsibility in completing the task

Delegation is a simple matter of personal preference. The biggest problem most leaders experience is their *lack of delegating*. Why do you delegate so seldom? Volumes could be written, but some basic reasons you don't delegate are that you are:
1. too thoughtless to ask yourself if someone else could do the task efficiently
2. too weak to recognize the myth of being totally self-sufficient—no one is!
3. too selfish to realize that no one gains by doing it all himself
4. too threatened to understand that others will not hate you for delegating work to them
5. too busy to analyze how much time can be gained for yourself while others accomplish those specific tasks
6. too stifled to cope with the reality that everyone makes mistakes—even perfectionists

7. too proud to accept the fact that doing everything yourself does not make you indispensable

You can properly delegate and learn to increase your efficiency, but first you must *agree to try* delegating authority. With some detailed terms, others will know exactly what they are to do and what results are anticipated. Here's how you can get the process of delegating on the right course:

1. Be Simple—explain in everyday language what's involved.
2. Be Specific—share the end results you anticipate.
3. Be Organized—outline the purpose of the task.
4. Be Instructive—show what you want done and how.
5. Be Enthusiastic—display confidence in their ability.
6. Be Creative—instill a desire for them to effectively perform.
7. Be Available—support and assist them continually.

Most of all, let them know you *trust* them to handle the task properly!

Delegating has been proven to work—why don't you try it?

HUMAN RELATIONS

Human relations is the development and maintenance of solid relationships between leaders, staff members, and peers.

Little do I have to say concerning the difficulty many pastors/leaders have with the art of understanding and getting along with people. In this day of complexity and great demands the need is greater than ever to develop good relationships with others. I believe we will always have a continual conflict in our society between the wants and desires of people and the principles of God's Word. Thus, the policies of your organization along with your personal management style may cause stress on some, while others simply conform.

Here are four fundamental concepts of human relations:
1. We live in a complex society.
2. We must accept the individual differences of others.
3. We should view others as God's most important asset.
4. We need to respect the dignity and values of others.

Now is the day to begin to develop and maintain good job relationships with your people, and between other leaders as well. I mention here "job relationships" because the system within most Christian organizations involves employees of the Master who are at this point supervised by you. We slip many times because others take the responsibility of serving the Lord lightly. Good human relations is a long, sometimes difficult process that only love, perseverance, and time will bring about. (This is not to belittle the power of prayer or limit the work of the Spirit.)

But you ask: "How do we cope with dissatisfaction?"

Create a sense of satisfaction! This may vary from one situation to another, but you can begin by reaffirming the decision your people made when they came to Christ. Next, remind them of the commitments they have made with God. Then, give them scripture concerning the crowns and rewards for faithful service. And last, but not least, show how great a privilege and honor it is to be His ambassador in this world. We are all enthusiastically motivated by what we are seeking, rather than by what we have. The *teamwork effort* of understanding and getting along with people, helping them to discover their own beautiful potential, is what creates true satisfaction.

In summary, remember your unique leadership position within the Body of Christ and seek to know every person as an individual. Provide what help you can to your people so they will achieve a measure of self-satisfaction! Begin to seek out ways of increasing everyone's commitment and contribution to the total framework of the organization.

Fostering a spirit of cooperation between and among each other is your greatest challenge in the human relations field. Your success is directly related to and dependent upon the performance of others. Determine right now to see each individual on their respective level and seek the Lord's guidance as you implement a life-style that reflects these principles. God will *bless* your efforts!

PRIORITIES

Priorities can be defined as objectives or activities arranged in order of importance. One of your most important concerns ought to be whether or not you are doing the right thing, in the right place, and at the right time. Or better yet, is *your organization* fulfilling these requirements?

Somehow, through the guidance of the Spirit, we must match the opportunities we have with the resources available to us. Is your organization "best fitted" for what you are presently doing? Or do you need to stop and evaluate your situation?

Since financial, material, and human resources are usually limited, you must prioritize your objectives. This is by far one of the most difficult tasks you face. There are no hard and fast rules. What works for me may not work for you even though it might for someone else.

The problem: establishing priorities is *largely a matter of opinion left open for criticism!* This is especially true for the Christian organization or church, since there are so many and varied demands placed upon them. But take heart, you can win this conflict. Remember, you must evaluate your present status. Are you:

1. doing the "right" thing?
2. in the "right" place?
3. at the "right" time?

Your staff and board need to set the pace and consistently maintain the course you've established. Without question, when you finalize your objectives in order of importance, someone's feelings will get hurt. Nevertheless, this must be done. The future of your ministry hinges upon your response to this great challenge!

MOTIVATION

Motivation is vital to leadership life-style. Basically motivation is defined as a person's needs or desires which cause him or her to act in a particular manner. Ideally, your organization should accomplish all of its objectives, and its members should satisfy all of their needs. Unfortunately this ideal isn't always achieved.

Contagious, Spirit-filled enthusiasm of great leaders has brought the Church through almost 2,000 years of ever-expanding influence and growth. Until recently, however, Christian leaders and pastors did not analyze employee motivation. In fact, business itself showed very little interest in motivation.

Today, changes have developed and psychologists have demonstrated that proper motivation is complex and very important. Significant theories of motivation have arisen, which directly apply to the practice of management. To touch upon modern concepts, let's look at Frederick Herzberg's two-factor theory.

When an individual feels *bad* about his position or job, he will usually relate it to salary, supervision, relationships, policies, working conditions, or basic security, all of which Herzberg describes as *extrinsic*. These factors are associated more with the "context" of the job than its "content." On the other hand, when an individual feels *good* about his job or position, he relates it to praise, promotion, or a sense of greater responsibility, etc. These factors are *intrinsic* because they relate more to the "content" of the job than to its "context." Thus, Herzberg has termed these factors *motivators,* because they seem to move people toward completion of their work more efficiently.

To better motivate your people, you should *enrich* the position or scope of their job rather than *enlarge* it. To enrich a person's job is to increase the amount of responsibility he is able to exercise in his work environment or overall ministry.

Christ never left anything undone but sought to enrich the life and scope of responsibility of those immediately around Him. Motivation was the key factor in how He dealt with men! Since motivation is frequently taught by a true example, Christ took every opportunity to enhance the learning process. He utilized the chain-reaction effect that proper motivation creates.

The inexhaustible nature of motivation is exciting! Someone has said that no change in behavior takes place purely unmotivated. When you are prompted to enrich your life and are influenced to act upon that prompting, you have been motivated. To motivate others, you must improve your relationship with them, set the example, and never give up, but continually seek new ways to enrich their ministry. Don't do for others what might motivate them to do for themselves and the Lord!

EMPATHY

Empathy is deep interpersonal communication. The very nature of empathy is often hidden in a maze of emotions, reactions, and fears. To be a successful leader, you should consider and develop this somewhat rare quality by looking deeply into the other person to see the world as he sees it.

Empathize for a moment by putting yourself in the place of the other person. Would you rather relate to someone:

- who really seeks to understand how you feel?
- who designs a working relationship that fits your needs?
- who sees that you don't really care to talk about a current issue just now, but helps you talk around it so you can make a logical, unemotional decision?
- who relates to you as a human being and interested friend?

Or to someone:

- who cares more about himself (pride) than he cares about your situations?
- who decides arbitrarily what will be done and tries to convince you that's what you really want?
- who implies that you are stupid for not planning ahead and/or a weak-kneed coward for not wanting to talk about the situation at hand?
- who sees you as just another employee and a possible financial loss?

Empathy is *feeling* what the other person is *feeling!* It is having a certain parallelism of life and a community of thought, a deep sensitivity of the heart for the other person. "How often I have looked up to find our thoughts, our feelings are the same!"

Empathy is not...
- feeling sorry for someone
- taking pity on someone
- feeling superior to someone
- putting someone down
- building someone up

To develop a genuine empathy in your ministry as a Christian leader, you must:

1. be able to accept yourself
2. be able to accept others as they are, without making self-imposed judgments
3. be able to let go of your own self-awareness, so you can take on an awareness of the other person
4. be able to understand what you are experiencing from the other person

And you need to be able to do all these things freely and naturally!

You cannot force empathy. You cannot "concentrate" and make empathy happen. Rather, you prepare yourself to experience empathy as God's Spirit works through your life. It's rather like water flowing downhill: "You cannot *make* it happen, you can only *let* it happen."

Now, in the power of God, empathize!

WRITTEN COMMUNICATION

Few things impress the community more about the quality of your organization or church than the quality of your communications. Major corporations use expensive equipment and insist on strict standards for the people who operate it, since one slipup could be very costly. While a professional appearance can be achieved with appropriate machines and accurate typists, the harder job is knowing how to make the printed material (or letter) read well.

Many schools of thought are available—some not the best. The usual advice to "write like you talk" is, I believe, completely wrong. Written and spoken rhythms are different; few people speak in complete sentences, while written material should be grammatically correct. Professional writers and advertisers spend hours reworking their material until both the language and the structure are satisfactory.

Seek a professional and competent approach for your communications. Here are a few rules to follow:

1. **Plan your letters**—Whether you prefer a written or mental outline, know what you want to say before you begin. Your points should follow in a logical order to produce the results you are after. Try telling the other person all he needs to know to react to your message intelligently—and no more.

2. **Get to the point**—Modern thinking indicates that you should start with the conclusion, even if you have to say no! Being honest up front, leaving little false hope, is best.

3. **Learn the guidelines of proper grammar**—Professional writers and English teachers consult reference books regularly; don't be too proud to do the same. Today's language is complex and changing, but most rules still apply. Keep up with the current style.
4. **Keep sentence structure simple**—It's good advice to vary the length of your sentences, very seldom exceeding 20-25 words.
5. **Keep paragraph structure simple**—The purpose of a paragraph is to develop one thought.
6. **Use simple vocabulary**—One of the marks of an amateur is the use of "fat phrases" and long words.
7. **Write with authority**—Use a firm and reassuring tone that displays confidence.
8. **Write with humor**—When appropriate, you can make your point with examples and people-related situations.
9. **Avoid cliches**—This is tougher than it sounds, because yesterday's clever phrase is too soon today's overstated expression.
10. **Use the first-person singular**—Current thinking prefers the pronoun "I" over the weaker expression "we."

Writing isn't an exact science. There's abundant room for creativity. The best advice is to organize your thoughts, then put them down on paper in the clearest way you can to achieve your desired result. As you think it through and proofread your content, your communication process will improve.

EXECUTIVE SKILLS

In the parable found in Luke 12:42-48, we are reminded of the two servants and their frightening dilemma. The faithful and wise servant (vv. 42-44) receives the appointment of leadership by rising from the ranks and because of his faithfulness becomes "ruler over all." On the other hand, the foolish and faithless servant described in verses 45-58 is motivated by the anticipation that "he will not get caught."

There are two principles of leadership demonstrated in the parable of Luke 12. First, the person who holds a position of leadership exercises a greater responsibility and will be accountable to the Lord for that responsibility. Second, since both servants shared the intitial responsibility to "know" the will of the master, both those who know God's will and do not do it and those who do not know God's will are punished because *both had the responsibility of knowing.*

Responsibility, then, is imperative! It's not a choice given in leadership roles. Responsibility, simply stated, is the willingness to make decisions (based upon data, experience, and the Word) and to stand true to them.

The responsibilities of leadership are not always pleasant. Frequently they represent **work which no one else is willing to do.** Your organization may have difficulty recruiting leaders because people simply do not want the responsibility.

Developing effective Christian leaders is not easy. But it is essential! Christian leadership is a style: *a life-style.* The most important aspect of style is reflected in how you as a leader view your subordinates. Three basic styles of leaders are:

1. **The Autocratic Leader**—feels that he alone can direct the activities of his subordinates satisfactorily, and that, because of his greater ability, all others must bend to his commands: a dictator's role.
2. **The Passive Leader**—adopts a nondirective style of leadership that indicates a middle-of-the-road approach. Such an individual shrinks from the basic responsibility of leadership and allows free rein within his sphere of control.
3. **The Democratic Leader**—seems to be the most favored in the late 20th century and is greatly supported by the New Testament. Such a leader is group-oriented and provides general supervision but never insists on his way.

As an effective leader, you must share the responsibility of decision making and overall planning, rather than forcing ideas. You become a member of the team, but not on an equal basis. Basically, you recognize your gifts and others' in order to fulfill the goals of your people and organization.

THE ULTIMATE EXAMPLE

It is my firm belief that Christ's primary goal was to have fellowship with the Father—that is, to keep the channels of communication open and live a pure life before men in order to fulfill the plan of salvation. You and I ought to pattern our life-style after our Lord's perfect example.

Please don't confuse Christ's "primary" goal with His "real" goal of ministering on earth. Notice, if you will, what the majority of His resources were used for:

1. Matt. 1:19-21—Angel appears to Joseph declaring Jesus' future ministry.
2. Luke 19:9-10—Jesus shares with Zacchaeus His ministry.
3. 1 Tim. 2:1-4—Paul bears witness of Jesus' ministry.

His real goal was "to seek and to save that which was lost." What a Man! Here was a first-class leader who managed people with an individualized concern. He knew how to make things happen, and He did! But He never lost sight of His real goal.

Somewhere in the maze of activities, work, home, sports, TV, friends, and family, we have lost the qualities our Lord possessed as a loyal Son entrusted with an awesome responsibility. The responsibility He had is ours today. To be like Him, we need to develop mature attributes as His managers within any organization or church. I can think of five particular qualities that every leader should possess:

1. **Persistence**—to stick it out until the job is finished
2. **Adaptability**—to "cope" with the external pressures
3. **Endurance**—to undergo hardships and frustration until the goal is reached
4. **Reliability**—to be dependable and predictable, always!
5. **Cooperation**—to submit to proper authority, while helping others

Begin now to rearrange the information in your mind in order to gain a better perspective and understanding of your role. By making these changes, your actions will represent sound management concepts and principles.

Positive results from the use of this book can be yours as you recognize that the *only limitation God has . . . is you!*

SUCCESS
(Achievement)

True success in your ministry is a matter of opinion—yours and the Lord's. He and you alone measure the degree of spiritual victory, as well as administrative success. Although much has been written on this topic, we can be guilty of ever learning and never doing what we ought to do. Apply new concepts in your ministry! The following ought to help you advance the cause of Christ as each becomes a way of living:

1. **Sharing**—Information reduces anxiety! The willingness to share your knowledge and skills with others is essential for greater effectiveness. If you seek to keep all things to yourself, you won't last long. Nobody likes a loner; sooner or later you will dig your own grave.

2. **Concern**—The love for people is essential, but only a genuine display of respect for individual needs and interests bears fruit. For you to get along with others successfully, you must be concerned about finding their quality points rather than exploiting their weak ones.

3. **Mistakes**—The ability to learn from mistakes and profit by them is vital to success. Thomas Edison once said, "Don't call your failures mistakes; call them an education." Everyone makes mistakes, but the difference between a successful and unsuccessful person hinges on the ability to never make the same mistake twice!

4. **Compromise**—The understanding that life itself is a bundle of compromises makes the big difference. You must be mature, flexible, and big enough to modify your views occasionally. Success is not built all alone, but by sharing experiences and giving in, at times, to those around us.
5. **Attitude**—To excel and advance in your respective field, you must have the "we" instead of "I" attitude. Successful people are more concerned with putting something "into effect" than with "who gets the credit." Your own success is largely dependent on others, and you will go further as a member of the team than you will on your own.
6. **Decisiveness**—The ability to make a decision on whatever can be accomplished at "the time" is the key here. If you refuse to make a decision until you have all the facts at your disposal to attempt that "perfect solution," you will go down with the ship!
7. **Proportion**—The ability to direct your attention toward what is "really" important will give you a proper sense of proportion. Many leaders are too busy being busy to accomplish anything. Treating every task the same will produce an imbalance in your administration and most likely you will not succeed.
8. **Confidence**—The knowledge and ability within you is what sells others on your capability to handle any responsibility or task. Developing confidence involves study, intense application, and the concept of putting forth your best each day. To accomplish true confidence in yourself takes consistent, old-fashioned hard work.

There's no formula for success that will work—if you don't.

3

POTENTIAL PROBLEMS

STRESS

Stress is a normal response to the pressures around you!

If you are about to be attacked by a murderer or mugged on the street, your body responds with a surge of adrenaline, furious pumping of blood, tensing of muscles, and heavy breathing. You are mentally and physically ready to fight or flee.

Symptoms of "fight" or "flight" also occur when we are not in physical danger. If you are about to preach or make a crucial presentation to your board, you may get "butterflies," trembling hands, perspiration, etc. Such responses aren't harmful when they last only a short while. If they subside immediately after such encounters, they've probably done no harm. In fact, if the stress was under control, you probably benefited from your state of alertness.

Stress, then, becomes harmful when it lasts longer than the pressure that caused it! The habitual response to persistent, undefined anxieties which are totally out of proportion to the pressure is what will drain you. For some, everyday events are enough to cause stress, while others thrive under pressure.

Without question, everyone responds differently. A hassle for one is a challenge to another. The key is knowing your own tolerance! To what degree does pressure make you work at *your best,* and when does it produce too much stress for you to handle? If you identify yourself as someone who is experiencing excessive stress and not adapting to it successfully, you can take several steps to reduce the problem. Along with prayerful renewal, there are two major remedies: (1) reduce stressful responses within; and (2) decrease pressure from without.

Even if you can reduce some pressures that cause stress, you can't eliminate them all. In fact, you wouldn't want to—without stress life would be dull! The goal is to keep stress to a level you can handle, so that it contributes to your productivity without leading to physical or mental illness.

Remember, to control stress you should:
1. Practice relaxation.
2. Watch for body signals.
3. Control your thoughts.
4. Get a hold on outside pressures.
5. Avoid overloading yourself.
6. Practice time management techniques.
7. Plan ahead.
8. Spend time doing what you want to do!

If you have little time for family, friends, and outside interests, your life is dangerously unbalanced. Make your ministry a *part of your life,* not *all* of it!

INACTIVE MEMBERS

How many members do you lose to inactive status every year?

It's not unusual. All churches and organizations lose members entirely or partially to the inactive files for various reasons. Few, if any, can afford to overlook the losses.

Inactive members represent a rich source of potential! Often, they are better prospects than the new names you turn up. Though some of your inactive members may have moved, etc., most of them still need you!

A quick and inexpensive way to *reach out* to inactive members is to maintain every name on your mailing list, and pull out the best possibilities to give them individual attention. Now, use the following steps to convert inactive members to active participants:

1. Find out why the inactive member dropped out

   To successfully reach such members, you must discover the reason for the loss. It may be something your people did or didn't do, or it may be something out of your control.

   When you know the reason, design your approach to overcome it. Often inactive members are taken for granted and simply overlooked. Let them be heard as you share how much they have been missed!

2. Investigate the inactive members' present situation

   Don't assume that their needs of several months or years ago still apply. The situation in their home may have changed! Once you know the circumstances, go with a solution or suggestions to encourage their involvement. Be open, honest, and understanding as you take a positive step in this direction.

3. Establish a nucleus of concerned people to make personal contacts

    What is the best way to get in touch with the inactive member—mail, telephone, a personal call? Nothing beats the personal, one-on-one visit in their home. If your investigation was adequate and your approach meets their need, you will most likely receive an encouraging reception. Set up a regular system with a dedicated nucleus, and go get 'em.

It is possible for large organizations to reach the inactive through direct mail. Create a new brochure with the inactive member in mind and enclose it with a carefully worded letter. Keep the tone friendly, the style informal, and the text short. You will get a greater response if you give each letter a personal touch (not a form letter) and if you send it first class. Remember, don't give up after a single try. The second time around include a questionnaire. Ask a few simple questions of opinion, leaving space for their answers. Most people will take the time to respond, especially if they believe you are really listening to their comments.

Inactive members are a rich source for obtaining active participants. Ask God to show you how!

COMPLAINERS

Do you run from or avoid the common complainer? You and your staff members may hope that things will straighten out if the person has time to simply cool off. Rarely does this tactic work. Delay in facing the issue usually makes the individual more tense and only complicates the situation.

The following guidelines will give you direction:

1. **Confront the Complaint**—Don't try to fool yourself or the complainer into thinking nothing is wrong. Let the person talk. Don't interrupt, even if you know what is wrong and how to handle it. When he is finished, you will have plenty of time to share and relate to him. Being heard is his first need.

2. **Pinpoint the Problem**—While the complainer is talking, your job is to try to understand the complaint. When he stops, your task is to restate the complaint as you understand it in order to verify your concept.

3. **Defuse the Situation**—Take the complainer's point of view. If you are at fault, you won't find it hard to take his point of view. You'll be genuinely sorry, whether or not you're personally to blame, and your apology will go a long way in calming the individual down.

   If it is clear that he is definitely at fault, you may find it more difficult to take his side; you're being blamed for his mistake. Yet you have nothing to gain by a blunt statement of the facts. Recognize that he is not aware of his mistake; he believes you're in the wrong.

You'll just have to correct his error, but with tact.

However you decide to remedy the problem, don't flatly tell him that he is wrong! If you do, it's certain to put him on the defensive, which may provoke the situation even more.

4. **Agree on a Solution**—Once you see the problem from his vantage point, work out a solution that satisfies him and take immediate action. If the situation can't be solved on the spot, start with the first step and work toward the ultimate solution.

5. **Go the Second Mile**—The complainer will appreciate your quick action to resolve his complaint but may still resent the original error, whether yours or his own. To remove any trace of ill feeling, offer to go beyond the problem by doing something extra.

The results?

The next time you ask him to assist you, he will remember your help instead of his complaint.

Too often the reason for general complaints within your organization stems from a basic lack of communication. When your people are better informed, everyone will work to develop a more harmonious atmosphere.

PROCRASTINATION

Many leaders say the end of the day comes surprisingly fast: so fast they hardly have time to finish any planned projects. There's rarely a minute when the phone doesn't ring, a crisis doesn't demand intervention, or a routine activity doesn't push toward a deadline. The common response even you sometimes give is a resolution to do better tomorrow. Yes, tomorrow you will clean up those tasks, big and small, which have been begging for attention for weeks.

Procrastination is the problem, not the lack of time. You have the ability to fit in every activity you are determined to accomplish. It's not easy to deal with this problem, but it can be overcome once you recognize it as the true culprit and stop blaming time.

Here's how you can kick the procrastination habit and accomplish more every day:

1. Keep your main objectives in mind—make a list of your goals and keep it in front of you as a daily guide.

2. Plan each day's work—before leaving the office, plan your activities for the following day and prioritize them according to importance.

3. Make notes to help plan your activity list—don't rely on memory, but take notes on anything requiring your attention.

4. Adjust your plans—use your peak efficiency hours to accomplish the most demanding tasks.

5. Set realistic deadlines—estimate how long it should take you to accomplish each task on your list.
6. Don't wait for inspiration—get started at once on your planned activity list each morning.
7. Overcome problems by finding a starting point—put your problem on paper and gather some general information to dispel your initial difficulty.
8. Make your decision and take action—indecision is nothing more than a waste of time.
9. Don't let time dictate the sequence you follow—stick to your priorities.
10. Control the outside interference—set aside regular times during which you accept only emergency calls. Ask your secretary to take messages from all other callers and instruct your staff to check with you later.

Although these tips will allow you to do more work, and hopefully more *important* work, some tasks require special approaches. Just because you have set up an activity list with priority labels, you won't necessarily complete every task you should do. Neglected jobs usually fall into two categories—the tedious and the intimidating. Here are a few more tips to help you accomplish these tasks as well:

1. Ask, "Why am I avoiding this task?" Once your difficulty is put into words, you'll find it easier to handle it.
2. Remember the benefits—once it's done, it'll be off your desk and your mind.
3. Break the job down—make a list of smaller steps which will generate momentum toward completion of the total job.
4. Make specific plans—define your basic strategy and make some decisions.
5. Take small steps—organize the facts and consider your options.

6. Recall similar projects of success—this should help you tackle current problems.

Implementing these principles at this point is the key. Can you really afford to procrastinate any longer?

CONFLICT

Interpersonal conflict is not always bad! Until I learned the truth of this statement, I was fearfully restricted as a manager. My administrative ability was stifled by that dark cloud of false impressions concerning conflict. My only view of it was negative. But what freedom can be ours when conflict is accepted as a creative way of growth and maturity. A learning process, when faced objectively, can and will be constructive!

Of course, the best way to overcome any conflict is to eliminate it before it happens. However, the battle often rages and we are caught trying to soften the blow. Here are five good concepts that can help solve those interpersonal problems:

1. **Decide** on a time and place to meet that is mutually agreeable.
2. **Direct** all anger and frustration on the crisis, not each other.
3. **Decipher** what the conflict is really about—analyze it more.
4. **Define** your position by being candid and honest.
5. **Don't** try to **win** during the crisis—never seek the upper hand.

Remember, two people are responsible for any relationship. As a leader and a Christian, you have a greater responsibility to the Lord. If you are struggling with an issue, ask God for sensitivity and seek to incorporate the five Ds into your thought pattern.

Many times in any situation we tend to slip into categories that lead to common interpersonal problems. Consider if you are guilty of any of these:
1. Overgeneralizing about others
2. Blaming others bluntly
3. Assuming others are incapable of change
4. Thinking you know what others are like
5. Failing to let others know what you expect of them
6. Expecting only one of two solutions to a problem

Too many times leaders fail to hear what people are really saying to them! The skill of listening may very well eliminate conflicts, but only as you employ it. As listening becomes more and more a part of your daily living, the feedback from others will serve as an indicator of the degree in which a conflict has been resolved. Stop, observe, and listen to what others are trying to say.

As a Christian, you must seek the power of the Holy Spirit to handle this area. Be a leader who follows His ever-present guidance and submits to His leadership. Bow your head with me even now and let's commit ourselves again to the cause of Christ. Let God instill these concepts and imbed them deep within your heart, that Satan might be defeated in the midst of every crisis or conflict you encounter.

Don't Forget: Conflict is not all bad. Creative conflict brings about more and more growth!

SOLUTIONS

Although growth results from conflict and crisis, we must have a method that will allow us to view the situation from another perspective. Thus, the principles outlined below will change your approach to solving any problem, but only as they become a part of your positive response.

I. **Analyze Your Situation**
   A. Collect and analyze all available data; ask yourself, "What is really happening?"
   B. Write out the problem; paraphrase in your own words what you feel are the important facts; give as much information as you think helpful in explaining the entire situation.
   C. Summarize the facts which are pertinent to your particular problem.
   D. A good and fair analysis will help you spot the problem quickly; do not overwrite; rather, pick only the facts necessary to define your problem and/or suggested solution. (Much of the information given will probably be "noise" and should be screened out.)

II. **Define Your Problem**
   A. State the problem and then further define as necessary; you can always list what might appear to be other problems involved, and then show why your choice is the main problem to be solved, before approaching the other issues.

B. *Do not* take for granted what appears to be the obvious problem; you may be simply restating the already identified outcome of mismanagement rather than the problem that caused the outcome.

III. **Evaluate Your Alternatives**
   A. Briefly state possible alternative solutions to the problem identified. What should you do? What can you do given the constraints of the problem or without further information?
   B. As you list each alternative, or following a listing of all the alternatives, evaluate the advantages and/or disadvantages of each.
   C. *Do not* limit yourself to alternatives suggested by others. Use your imagination and any other knowledge gained from past experience which appropriately applies to the problem.

IV. **Recommend Your Solution(s)**
   A. Simply state which alternative(s) you recommend as the best solution(s).
   B. Justify that choice and explain how you are going to implement your solution; give the steps needed and how long it should take.

Important Reminder: Keep this in simple form with short statements under each heading. The more you practice this very brief method of problem analysis, the better your results will be in the role of an effective manager.

4

PROMOTIONAL STRATEGY

ADVERTISING

Advertising is many things to many people. Beyond a doubt, advertising is everywhere, with the average American adult being bombarded with over 400 advertising messages a day. In short, advertising is an attempt to communicate information to others, so take advantage of every opportunity and occasion to reach out to others in your community. Be different! *Attract attention!*

As a leader and manager, you must be aware that advertising plays an important part in the life of any organization. Never underestimate the power of sharp and well-prepared advertising material: Big business doesn't. They know from experience that proper advertising is powerful, and they prove it every day. Don't be afraid to put some of the principles in this section to work right away.

I. A BIBLICAL BASIS FOR ADVERTISING
   A. Jer. 50:2—"Declare ye among the nations, and *publish*, and set up a standard; *publish*, and conceal not."
   B. Luke 14:23—"And the lord said unto the servant, Go out into the highways and hedges, and *compel them* to come in, that my house may be filled."
   C. Acts 2:6—"Now when this was *noised abroad*, the multitude came together" (all italics added).

II. THE PURPOSE OF ADVERTISING
   A. To inform people about your organization and its program

B. To attract these same people and produce action
  C. To see growth in Christians and members
  D. **To win the lost**—Evangelism is our ultimate Goal

III. SOME SUCCESSFUL ADVERTISING IDEAS
  A. Organization Members (as a resource)
  B. Telephone Calls
  C. Bulletins
  D. Radio/TV (Public Service Announcements)
  E. Posters, Flyers, and Inserts
  F. Direct Mailings/Newsletters
  G. Business Signs/Billboards
  H. Complimentary Tickets

IV. HELPFUL HINTS FOR PRINTED MATERIALS
  A. Format: layout appearance and neatness
  B. Quality: paper stock, reproduction, and color
  C. Content: accurate, complete information and proper spelling

V. RESOURCES FOR MORE IDEAS
  A. Magazines
  B. Newspaper Ads
  C. Yellow Pages
  D. Other Churches/Organizations
  E. Input and Feedback from Others

VI. YOU MUST HAVE SOMETHING TO ADVERTISE
  A. Improve on what you already have
  B. Seek new ways to build your programs and events

The necessity of prayer in preparation for any event, including the regular activities, is of vital importance. All the planning and advertising (no matter how well done) will fail without remembering the power of prayer (2 Chron. 7:14).

AD IDEAS

Never assume that people will seek out your programs and special events simply because "they are there." Ideas are funny things—they don't work unless you do! The rest of this section is of absolutely no value unless you are willing to direct others into these channels of usefulness:

I. PERSONAL INVITATION
The most effective invitation is *the face-to-face, friend-to-friend variety.* If your own people are enthusiastic, they will bring their friends to a special event. This is always the key to greater attendance.

II. TELEPHONE CALLS
Never underestimate the persuasive power of a simple phone call, which is the next best thing to a personal invitation.

III. BULLETIN
Use a bulletin for at least a month in advance in order to build the interest among those already involved. The inserts should be printed in sharp colors, bold type, and with style.

IV. RADIO/TELEVISION
You can contact thousands of listeners in a moment with radio and television advertising.

Radio time is free when you have the announcement read on the station's "Community Billboard" or public service section. Every station is required to have a set time (certain number of minutes) each day for public announcements.

Television is the best and most effective media in which to advertise, but it is also the most expensive. Ten- or 20-second spots three days in advance of the event are sufficient.

V. POSTERS/FLYERS

Printed materials are a constant reminder of an upcoming event from the time they are printed until the special event day. When strategically placed, they are a very effective and inexpensive way to advertise.

A. Include the date, time, place, and any cost.
B. Make posters readable at a distance.
C. Place posters in good public locations, with permission.
D. Always remove them after the event is over.
E. Flyers may be used as handouts, posters, or mailers.

VI. DIRECT MAIL

Advertising experts claim that direct mail advertising gets better results per dollar spent than any other form of advertising. The people you mail to should include the key individuals involved in local church groups, neighbors, civic organizations, as well as your own members. Always seek to build your mailing list up every year. Remember to accompany the flyers or printed material with a letter of endorsement by a prominent individual or pastor for a more effective mailing combination.

A mailing at three weeks prior to and another the week of your event will bring the greatest rewards.

VII. BUSINESS SIGNS/BILLBOARDS
Often owners of businesses in the community have signs on which short announcements can be spelled out, such as: THE BELIEVERS QUARTET, 7:00 p.m., Sunday, October 1, IMMANUEL CHURCH.

On some occasions, billboard companies will offer advertising space at a minimal cost, in which your billboard message will appear on a rotation basis throughout the city or region. The regular monthly billboard rental is very, very costly.

VIII. COMPLIMENTARY TICKETS
Everyone loves to get something for nothing! The recipient of a complimentary ticket feels a definite urge to attend the event (even if there is no charge).

Remember, advertising has no value until
it is in front of others, constantly!

NEWSLETTERS

... the one and only thing you do to touch every member in the church!

Don't allow your newsletter to be so routine!

Purpose:	**Steps to Success:**
1. Inform	1. Research/investigation
2. Promote	2. Plan/set goals
3. Report	3. Implementation/getting it out
4. Uplift/inspire	4. Evaluation/looking it over
5. Survey	

Content:

Should undergird the total program of the church. Be as original as possible. Make everything *focus* on your church, even if borrowed.

Make the newsletter specific and to the point, or it will die because of generality. Emphasize unique features:

—Report on people, not programs.

—Dramatize dull statistics.

—Localize denominational programs (visualize).

—Personalize people in church (not staff).

The *pastor's column* should set the tone and mood for the church and give perspective, objectives, and goals of leadership. Plus, it:

—should be done weeks in advance

—needs to deal with issues and specific needs

- —should give the "why" and biblical view for ministries of the church
- —may tackle controversy as he would never do in services
- —prepares congregation for the next Sunday's message
- —deals with members as responsible disciples

Suggestion:
Always use more photos of people over all other art or filler.

Design:
- —Typesetting gives more to the page.
- —Upgrades priority of reader.
- —Short articles need small pages, large articles need broad sides.
- —Everything the church does should have personality to match it!
- —Uniformity:
    1. Use same typeface on all variety for reinforcement.
    2. Your eye is attracted to the heavy print on a page.
    3. Limit the amount of heavy print for maximum coverage.
    4. Human eye reads 39 characters per line; never go below 20 characters per line (10 pt. average).

How to Write:
- —Don't exaggerate; go for honest appraisals.
- —Historical setting (using weekly column).
- —Tie every article to relative thoughts/people.
- —Be brief, quick, clean, clear.
- —Format should be geared to your church size and design.
- —Use human interest appeal!

Format:
- "Less is more!"
- The simpler the design, the more likely the content will be read.
- *Zone cues* (a marker/flag which provides a contrast to catch the eye).
- Headlines.
- Rules and borders.
- White space (should be artistically placed.)

I. Move toward content; the message is what counts

II. Keep the format simple and durable

III. Remain consistent in format
   - Everything "flush left—flush top"; you can leave space at the bottom
   - Ragged right is easier on the eye and not so costly! It's OK!
   - Informal balance is just as acceptable as formal balance!

IV. Work *with* the fold of the paper and not against it. (Otherwise you create visual noise.)

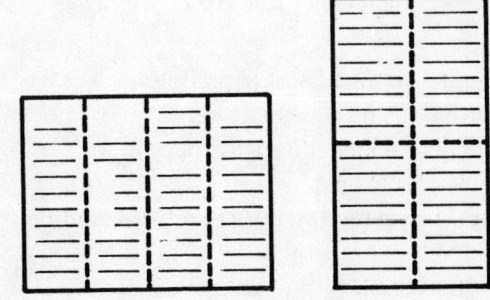

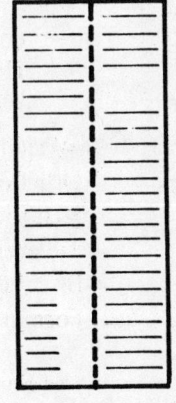

V. Never use more than two styles of type in one printed piece.
   —Ratio of headlines to body type is important. They must be larger, at least twice as bold as body type (should look like a crane carrying strings of type).
   —The more complicated the typeset, the fewer characters you should use.
   —Upper and lower case is much easier to read than all caps.
   —Identity (variation of small details plus familiarity).
   —A signature personalizes content and makes it real!

HELPFUL HINTS

Camera-ready Layout Copy

1. Clean typewriter before typing final copy for a good clean finish.
2. When preparing a final copy, always use black ink on white paper for the best offset printing results.
3. When centering titles/headings on the typewriter:
   A. Place on center.
   B. Back space 1 for every 2 strokes.
   C. Then type.
4. Remember when typing that:
   PICA has 10 spaces to the inch and
   ELITE has 12 spaces to the inch.
   Example: 3-inch width column
   Pica=30 spaces
   Elite=36 spaces
5. A carbon typewriter ribbon gives the best reproduction.
6. Cut out any items to use in paste-up from other sources not copyrighted.
7. Create a filing system to store "clip art" for future use.
8. Check local office supply stores and graphic arts shops for rub-off letters, borders, backgrounds, clip art, and other artist helps to give your newsletter eye appeal. Graphic art subscription services are also available from various sources. Check your Yellow Pages.

9. Fillers—may be typed ahead of time and filed by length size. When you need a 1-inch filler, just pull it from the 1-inch file, etc.

10. A light table is the easiest way to do layout. Remember, you can make your own for almost nothing, but be sure to use a fluorescent bulb.

PLAN SHEET

Goal or Objective: _____
_____
_____
_____

Who: _____
_____
_____

What: _____
_____
_____

When: _____
_____
_____

Where: _____
_____
_____

Why: _____
_____
_____

5

PERSONNEL STRUCTURE

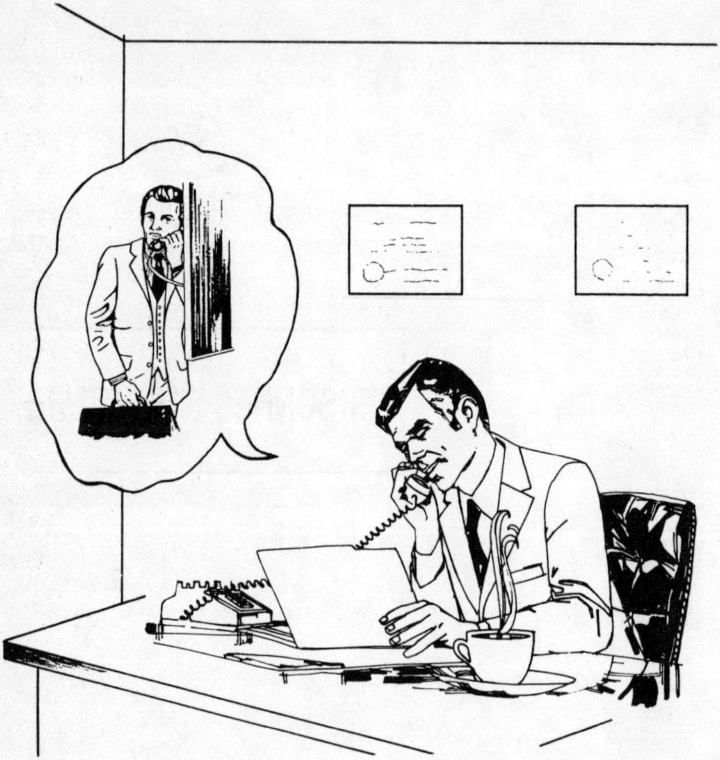

HIRING

You may be the vital person in your organization, but you can't oversee every function. You must depend on one or more key people to shoulder some of the responsibility.

When you endeavor to hire key staff members or employees, you must establish a system for getting the best possible person. Though you believe God knows your particular need, it is imperative to utilize all the available resources.

You may *not* think of yourself as an expert in personnel procedures, but your administrative judgment and managerial skills will give you competence for successfully screening and selecting candidates. The following factors will enable you to recommend the key people your church/organization should hire:

I. Clarify the nature of the position

   Before you begin your search for the right person, you should define the nature of the job. Consider the value of composing a job description to simply clarify the basic duties. Remember to define the major function and list the tasks involved. Also, include the policy on compensation and benefits.

II. Consider the background and necessary skills

   Seek the individual whose background and skills best meet your needs. Don't ask for more than you need.

   Must an individual have a specific degree or be a seminary graduate? See if you can discover the applicant's character and judge him on specific abilities.

With this in mind, don't make your requirements too specific. The more general you make your basic requirements, the less likely you are to eliminate potentially valuable staff members.

III. Carefully screen resumés

For a key staff member who will work directly with you, it pays to screen resumés yourself! Here are three techniques that will assist your preliminary screening.

　A. **Examine** each one for your basic requirements, looking for those redeeming features that could make an interview worthwhile.

　B. **Evaluate** neatness and legibility—a smudged, hastily written, or poorly typed resumé could be a clue to careless work habits.

　C. **Expect** a complete and thorough resumé. Any period of time glossed over may cause you to wonder what the candidate is hiding.

IV. Correctly handle the personal interview

The most important part of the selection process is the personal interview, which should be conducted by you.

　A. Schedule an uninterrupted conference in a private location. You'll learn more about a candidate in 10 concentrated minutes than in an hour split into several confusing segments.

　B. Review the resumé just prior to your interview. Scan it ahead of time, noting questions you have, statements that need elaboration, and points that should be investigated.

　C. Put the candidate at ease. After the initial greeting, offer the individual a chair, coffee, and exchange a few words before getting down to business.

　D. Encourage the candidate to share and exchange conversation. The purpose of the interview is to discover the right person for the position, and this can only be achieved from the information *you receive*—not from the information you give.

E. Give the candidate your total attention. Concentrate on what is said, and perhaps on what is not said.

F. End unproductive interviews quickly. Don't prolong the meeting, but simply end the interview pleasantly and quickly.

G. Allow the candidate an opportunity to ask questions. Once the individual convinces you of his ability, offer some more specifics and answer any questions he may have. When you depart, tell the candidate the next step to expect and when he will hear from you.

V. Channel your information to the personnel committee for recommendation

The committee should carry your recommendation further by (1) checking references, (2) meeting with the candidate, (3) investigating deeper in past experiences, and (4) making final recommendation to your board and/or voting members. Also, allow an opportunity for the candidate to meet your total membership.

IV. Call the candidate and inform him of the membership's decision

Schedule another conference to finalize the decision and relate policies, benefits, and salary agreed upon. Introduce the candidate to other employees and orient him with some degree of detail.

God's choice should be your main concern! Seek His leadership and guidance in the overall process, while asking for a spirit of sensitivity.

JOB DESCRIPTION

Date _____

Name _____

Title _____

Purpose of Job:
(What needs to be accomplished) _____

_____

_____

_____

Duties of Job:
(A detailed list of tasks) _____

_____   _____

_____   _____

_____   _____

_____   _____

_____   _____

Relationship within Job:
(Who is responsible to whom) _____

_____

_____

Qualifications for Job:
(Abilities/talents needed to do the job well) _____

_____

_____

Proposed Training Opportunities:

_____

_____

STAFF PRODUCTIVITY

Boredom and *lack of involvement* in the total program of your organization are the most common symptoms of nonproductive staff members. Many problems may be interrelated, causing a staff member's "lack of interest" to surface. Here is how you can increase productivity and better involve an individual staff member:

1. **Directly ask** him for suggestions as to how his ministry could be more interesting and at the same time do more for the church/organization. Be sure to observe him over a period of time—you'll be surprised how much better you understand his suggestions.

2. **Continue showing interest** in him and his ministry. Once you lose interest in someone, he will lose interest in himself! Circulate among your staff, asking about possible problems and suggestions. Listen to their ideas and show you care for them as people.

3. **Recognize a job well done!** Anyone likes to receive credit when it is deserved, and so does your staff member. If you understand him individually, your recognition will be more effective as you: *(a)* boost his ego, *(b)* enlarge his office area, *(c)* assign him a new project, or *(d)* purchase a new book for him. If a deserved wage increase or bonus is in order, recommend it to the board or personnel committee for approval.

4. **Create new interest** within your organization. Rotate some routine tasks to others, suggest a special day off,

or buy staff members lunch on various occasions. Possibly a day off each week could stimulate a fresh interest. Take almost any staff suggestion and try it!

5. **Share your managerial decisions** with your staff and keep them informed of upcoming events. Demonstrate that you value their individual contributions, and you will automatically reinforce their sense of security.

6. **Set goals** and maintain high standards for your staff. If they feel you are lax and uncommitted, they are likely to take the easy route. Don't display a negative approach, but rather, show every person that you consider them highly capable and hardworking. If they fail to fulfill your expectations on a consistent basis, prayerfully seek their inner thoughts as you sit down together to discover God's will in their ministry. A team concept is the only answer for successful "Total Management."

Your nonproductive staff members may do more than just become bored and dissatisfied; they may contaminate others in your organization with their negative attitudes. So, it is vital to know your staff and find the best ways to motivate them. Ask the Lord for direction and an open mind as you implement these principles.

Have you stopped to simply listen to what your staff has to say? The odds are great that some very good solutions will be verbalized and your answer will be very clear: Go to it!

SECRETARIES

Beside every outstanding Christian leader you will find a qualified secretary who has a sensitive grasp of her boss's needs and who helps him function through good organization and scheduling. Look for a secretary who will truly be your assistant—and see that she has that title!

In determining how your secretary measures up as an assistant, you might ask yourself these questions:

1. Does she possess necessary secretarial skills?
2. Does she know your schedule and help you keep appointments?
3. Does she keep the office running smoothly in your absence?
4. Does she respect confidential information?
5. Can you assign her a task and then be secure in the knowledge she will follow through on it?
6. Is she loyal to you and your organization?
7. Does she suggest helpful ideas or procedures and use her initiative and creativity in meeting her responsibilities?
8. Does she know the difference between an urgent task and an important one? Are her priorities the same as yours?

If you can answer yes to these questions, you have an exceptional assistant! This section will give you some practical suggestions for establishing and maintaining a healthy working relationship.

Tips to help your secretary perform more effectively:
1. Work ahead—don't give her stacks of work that all need to be done by "yesterday."
2. Communicate! Keep her well informed.
3. Trust her with your whereabouts. Let her know when you leave the office and when you can be expected back. (It is NOT necessary for her to share this information with callers, but SHE needs to know to do her job well.)
4. Organize your work before you begin to delegate it. Think out your letters before you begin to dictate.
5. Allow her the freedom to make decisions within the realm of her responsibility. Trust her judgment.
6. Get her input on office procedures, equipment, and other relevant matters. She is closer to these areas than any other staff member.
7. Provide a pleasant atmosphere to work in.
8. See that proper office equipment, reference materials, etc., are available for her to do the job that is expected of her.
9. Encourage her participation in seminars and secretarial courses.
10. Show appreciation for work well done!

An efficient secretary can handle a multitude of responsibilities for you. Consider delegating these tasks to her:
1. Attend meetings; take notes and summarize proceedings for you
2. Plan meetings, send notices, prepare resource papers
3. Handle travel arrangements
4. Screen applicants for office positions
5. Reply to correspondence—"Write so and so and tell him such and such" may be all you have to say to answer many letters

6. Trust her to send letters that go out over your signature—why use your time reading every letter you dictate?
7. Meet with sales representatives
8. Schedule appointments
9. Make and receive phone calls regarding both routine and not-so-routine matters
10. Scan reading materials for information helpful to your ministry

Encourage your secretary to grow in her profession! If there is a secretaries' association in your area, by all means encourage her participation. Create an open relationship of respect and trust in your secretary—expand her scope of responsibility.

Many executives will testify that their most valuable staff member is their secretary. Find that most valuable staff member that is *THE* assistant for you!

PERSONNEL HANDBOOK

A good personnel handbook can go a long way toward insuring a smooth office operation. More than any other tool, your handbook can prevent misunderstandings between employees and staff. If you have more than 10 employees, it can save a great deal of time in simply answering routine questions while saving budget money in relationship to overtime and paid expenses.

To be the most effective, a personnel handbook must be comprehensive to all who work with you, right down to your newest staff member. It should avoid technical language, difficult or undefined words, and complex sentences. Each section should be clear and self-evident.

Your handbook should also be attractive. In order to get others to read and refer to it when questions arise, make it easy to read and consult. *Attractive* doesn't mean *expensive*, with slick paper and color work. But it does need good design, with clean, modern typeface, proper white space on each page, and an occasional drawing or chart to break up the print.

Furthermore, your handbook needs to be kept up-to-date. When anything is outdated, it's useless! A practical suggestion is to assemble the pages in a loose-leaf binder so you can replace pages with new policy changes.

Finally, your manual must be complete. Every essential item should be covered. The nature of your organization will dictate the contents, but all personnel handbooks ought to include the following:

1. **Office Hours**—Make it clear and simple from the very beginning. Don't hesitate to specify length of lunch time or details concerning breaks. The general employees of your organization need the positive encouragement of what you expect in regard to daily schedules. (Overtime should be dealt with as well in this section.)

2. **Holidays and Vacations**—State which holidays you are going to observe and how many are paid. Explain your way of handling weekend holidays and whether or not you offer a substitute day. In like manner, detail your vacation policy. Spell out procedures, scheduling, and length of time off per year.

3. **Sick and Personal Leave**—Whatever you decide to impose, record it. Use a positive approach to enforce the meaning of "sick leave"—which ought to mean just that, or you may have employees treating it as extra vacation time.

   Additionally, some organizations give several days a year for personal leave, allowing employees to handle family problems or care for situations that cannot be handled after office hours.

4. **Leave of Absence**—If an individual wants an extra week of vacation or needs extended time away, you may want to allow it without pay. Don't forget to emphasize how long a leave may be, how long a period of employment is required to qualify, and the desired notice time.

5. **Pay Schedule**—Specify the frequency of paychecks and the time of day as well. Whether you hand out checks in the morning or later in the day, state a time and stick to it.

6. **Fringe Benefits**—Usually, medical and life insurance in whole or in part is basic. Make sure your employees understand exactly what their benefits are—it will improve morale immensely!
7. **Paid Expenses**—Establish a very clear understanding for expenses that are job related. Specify the kinds of expenditures that are permitted and who must approve them. Travel expenses are usually covered at a fixed amount per mile for those driving their own car. Details for such expenses belong in your manual.

The list of minor details is endless. Pick the few that affect you the most, or are important to you personally, and set forth procedures that best meet your church/organizational needs. Keep your personnel handbook in order and construct its content in a positive, enthusiastic way.

6

PREVENTATIVE ACTION

CREATIVE CHANGE

Your organization is changing! Growth, new programs, external pressures, and even competition from cults are forces which alter your methods or structure.

Such change may be as simple as a reassignment of duties or the deletion of certain programs. It may be as complicated as changing hands in leadership or the construction of an entirely new facility. But whatever the purpose, the anticipated benefits of change are seldom fully realized. It may take years for some of your people to function effectively in the new plan of action or accept the cost of making the change. Human anxieties are often very great.

With proper consideration and handling, the costs of change can be reduced. Look for a moment at some factors that contribute to the difficulties of making changes:

1. The basic plan structure
2. The possible status changes
3. The lack of proper communication
4. The unrealistic compensation of employees
5. The failure to give others *all* the information

The greatest single problem is that Christian leaders, like yourself, do not realize that every organization consists of people whose personal goals, values, makeup, and social relationships must be taken into account. These qualities do not belong to you and your immediate staff alone! Any plan that you initiate apart from this personality framework has little chance for success.

To achieve any goal (see section on goals) requires the paying of some price. Thus, it would be unrealistic for you to design a plan of change which requires a price higher than you are willing to pay. Plus, it is also important to take into account the capacities and limitations of other key people and the impact of the change on them.

These comments are frequently made when change is suggested: "We've never done it that way before"; or, "Don't suggest that now because people are too uptight." Even without these attitudes present, changes are resisted because of the *risk* that they may upset people.

FACT: Changes generally undertaken when people are upset not only *succeed;* they usually improve overall morale.

Would you believe that the greater the external pressures, the more realistic change you can undertake? But remember, you and your staff need to uphold the proposed changes in prayer, while keeping sensitive to the Spirit of God. The calm inner peace of the Lord will give the assurance of when to take action. Timing is vital!

While setting up a timetable for change, keep in mind that everything does not have to be done at once. Usually the basic foundation for change is laid, with a long-term objective in mind, so that the entire organization can phase into the total plan.

Like conflict, resistance is not always bad. It very well may point you to certain adaptations needed in the new plan. There are many forces involved in the opposition to making a change. The primary one is simply *human attitudes* which are reflected in one or all of the following:

1. Your people have not understood the importance of the proposed change.
2. Your people are not sure what will be expected of them if the change is made.

3. Your people probably feel somewhat threatened by such a change.
4. Your people do not know how to change.

You can reduce the forces of opposition by establishing an atmosphere of confidence, while presenting the new plan in a way that is understandable and wins approval. This, of course, is accomplished through the use of good communication skills and proper persuasion.

Change is difficult. Just the same, you can break those deeply ingrained habits and develop new ones through proper planning, perseverance, and prayer. Apply the principles and give God the praise for the positive results!

POLICIES

Why establish a Policy Manual? For one specific reason: to let your staff and employees know what is expected of them.

A good policy manual will insure a smoother operation of your entire organization or church. More than any other tool, a manual of this nature can prevent misunderstandings between you and your staff. A policy manual will save you a great deal of time answering routine questions, as well as money, by spelling out guidelines.

In order to produce the maximum amount of these benefits and more, your policy manual must be comprehensible to everyone in your organization. Remember to avoid technical language and religious jargon, difficult words and complex sentences. Make every line self-evident, with simple words, short sentences, and straightforward paragraphs.

Create an attractive manual! If you expect others to read it thoroughly and refer to it whenever the need arises, it must be easy to read and consult. I didn't say "expensive." It doesn't need photography, slick paper, or color work. But good design is a must. Make it clean, with a modern typeface, sufficient spacing, and occasional drawings, graphs, or charts to break up the type.

Keep your manual up-to-date. If it becomes outdated, it is absolutely *useless.* Assemble the pages in a loose-leaf format so you can replace old pages with new ones each time you make revisions. Seek to make your manual all-inclusive and bathe this endeavor in prayer. (See section on "Personnel Handbook.")

GROWTH

In order to experience growth, you must recognize the hazards and effectively deal with them. Growth in any organization is somewhat of a mystery, especially when you consider the various factors involved.

Think for a moment about the national statistics on churches. Ninety-five percent of the churches in America average under 340 in their morning worship service. Fifty percent average under 75. If your church has even 76 in attendance next Sunday morning, you would be *above average*.

So what keeps churches small—or for that matter, what keeps any Christian organization smaller than its potential? Circumstances and special situations may be a factor for some, but not for the vast majority.

If you are *not* experiencing growth, chances are your organization displays one or more of these characteristics:

1. The **Wrong Priority**—Take away the major thrust of evangelism or assign different-than-evangelism priority, and you have already failed. In general, such churches and organizations are not among the leaders in growth!

2. The **Lack of a Plan**—If you are not experiencing growth, it's probably because you haven't planned to! If you shoot at nothing, you will hit it every time.

3. A **Preoccupation with Finances**—Simply stated: It costs to grow and few are willing to pay the price. You

must take that step of faith if you want God to bless. It's necessary. If your organization is waiting until it can "afford" to grow, you will still be where you are at this time next year.

4. The **Traditional Program**—Growth will come as your message remains consistent, while your method constantly changes to make your message known. The famous seven last words of the church are: "We've never done it that way before."

5. The **Problem of Apathy**—The failure to properly direct people to serve Christ enthusiastically through your organization means little or no growth. "Where there is no vision, the people perish" (Prov. 29:18).

Growth is a matter of the heart and a determination of the will to accomplish the purpose of the Lord through the guidance and power of the Holy Spirit. In no way are the above characteristics exhaustive. You may or may not experience all of them, and sometimes a few are found even in growing churches to some degree. However, when you see these signs, beware of the hazards ahead. Since you are in command, you must cautiously guide your people out of the ruts and safely down the road to prosperity.

By God's grace, you as a sensitive Christian leader can do it!

DEVELOPMENT

Development involves the process of establishing priorities, building a program, identifying leadership, developing plans/goals, sharpening stewardship techniques, improving communications, training staff and employees, and providing objectives, counsel, and sound judgment.

A larger and deeper ministry means more projects of broader scope that all seem urgent. Almost daily you are pressed with the question of priorities. Long-range plans are slowly submerged in the wave of daily routine.

Occasionally, you need to evaluate your total program to recognize and clarify priorities. Here is an overview of the right priorities for efficient development:

1. **Public Relations**—the essential priority! If this area is weak, all other areas will suffer. Never underestimate this number one *cause,* since all others are the *effect.*

2. **Enlistment**—the underlying purpose of every Christian organization. Whether it's the Sunday School of a church, the registrar of a college, or the personnel director of a hospital, all are in the enlistment business.

3. **Stewardship**—the necessary ingredient for continued success. You must educate your people in this matter in a way that deals with their dollars and makes sense. With the Word, prayer, and faith you can drastically change motives and attitudes, which will reap results!

Ministry is the single word that should best describe the philosophy of your development program. In essence, this means you are primarily a "people" raiser, not simply a developer or fund raiser. The best approach for your membership is that of a genuine effort to help them to become better stewards in *every area* of their lives. This in turn will support your total development strategy.

There is no substitute for, there is no shortcut to, adequate long-range planning and a careful balance of priorities. With a scriptural approach and practical application, your development program will become God's delight.